FURTHER TALES FROM THE TIP

by

Peter McElhinney

To Duncan,
Best Wishes
Pete McElhinney

Illustrations by *'Mike'*

Also by Peter McElhinney

Tales from the Tip

Published 1996 by Avon Books
1 Dovedale Studios
465 Battersea Park Road
London SW11 4LR

ISBN 0-9531805-0-6

Published by

MP

Macum Publishing
Sale, Cheshire.

Typeset and Printed by
Short Run Print
Cheadle Hulme, Cheshire.

1.

The vision of Florence Gloob

Gloobs are the strangest little things you are ever likely to come across. Of course, you are not likely to come across them because they are very, very shy of human beings.

I think that is very sensible when you think of how some humans behave.

The only Gloob colony that I know about lives on a special Corporation Tip. Now, Corporation Tips are dangerous, so for the Gloobs' sake and your safety I will keep its location a secret.

Gloobs, like humans, come in all sizes and colours. Being different some how worries humans but it does not worry Gloobs.

They are just like little balls of coloured wool with sharp, but very polite ears. They have very long noses which do not cause them or anyone else the slightest bit of trouble. Their hands are the most helpful you will find anywhere. Their feet are delightfully enormous, which is just as well because they do not have any legs, at least not so as you would notice. Large feet prevent the unpleasant habit of rolling away in the middle of a conversation.

Before living on the tip, they lived in a rhubarb patch, probably because it was their favourite food. There they could go about bare footed but the tip was a different place altogether. It was dirty and had lots of sharp, dangerous, hidden things. They soon learned that they had to wear boots.

Living on the tip brought them into close contact with human beings - which they thought were very strange creatures. But humans did protect their feet and so the Gloobs learned, amongst other things, how to make boots.

Some of them began to have other ideas too, like Florence Gloob.

Florence Gloob suddenly had a vision (that is a sort of picture in your mind that you can actually see with your eyes open). It happened after a dislodged wooden box of old books fell on her.

She woke up ten minutes later to find her little world had disappeared. She appeared to be in a mystical tent. Above her floated a very small human in a strange uniform.

"Hello," greeted Florence but the small human being did not reply or move. It smiled benignly (difficult word that but it means nicely I suppose) it smiled benignly into the distance.

Florence read the words that fluttered round the vision.

"National Health Service," she read, "your future secured in looking after the health and welfare of the sick. There are many rewards in being a trained nurse. For further details, ring.....(and the rest was covered in mud).

Suddenly, a gust of wind blew the pamphlet high into the air and away. The bright sunlight made Florence shut her eyes tightly.

She could still see the smiling figure in her mind.

"That's it," she said, opening her eyes slowly, "I'm going to be a nurse and look after the sick."

She raced home to tell her father.

"WHAT!" he exclaimed, his old fur standing on end.

"I'm going to be a nurse," announced Florence.

"What is a nurse?!" thundered Florence's father. He wanted his daughter to be like other girl Gloobs and do practically nothing.

Florence closed her eyes to remember the words in her vision.

"A nurse looks after the health and welfare of the sick," she enlightened him (that means making it very clear to him so that even he could understand).

"Gloobs don't get sick," retorted her father, "or very rarely and then we look after ourselves."

"There are many rewards in being a trained nurse," said Florence, a mystical look on her face.

"Trained?"

"Well of course I'll have to train myself," said Florence, "I don't suppose you could get sick, could you?"

"When?" demanded her father, "this minute? Or would you prefer three o'clock this afternoon?"

"I've got to get a uniform first," Florence explained.

"You are talking a lot of nonsense, Florence Gloob!" her father told her, "and you are to forget this ridiculous idea immediately!"

"Or would you prefer three o'clock this afternoon?" Florence asked, a glazed look in her eyes.

Her father gave up and stormed away. Florence watched her father go, sadly, and then completely forgot everything except her burning ambition to be a nurse.

A little distance away was a blue pram lying upside down without any wheels. So far, no Gloob had claimed if for a house because it was rather large and dark inside.

"Now that," thought Florence to herself, "would make a wonderful hospital. But I must get a uniform first."

Gloobs do not really have to wear clothes, any more than an Angora rabbit does, or a Persian cat - and they are very fluffy. I have also hinted that Gloobs do not have legs of any significance (that means sort of any importance) so they do not wear trousers. Neither do they have waists around which they can put a belt. However, Florence insisted that she wanted a uniform.

Wearing a hat was no problem, so she began with that.

"It has to be white," she told her friend Cicely Gloob, "with a little red cross on the front."

Florence had searched the tip for the pamphlet with the photograph on it but had not been successful. Finally, just as she was about to give up, she found the torn out page of a toy catalogue and there was a nurse. She was looking at the picture of a doll dressed up in what looked like a large white handkerchief on its head with a red cross on the brow. Over a blue dress, the doll wore a white pinafore also with a red cross on it.

Florence showed the picture to Cicely.

"That should not be difficult," said Cicely, "I'll have to make it out of paper though."

Florence was sure that would be all right.

It took five minutes to make. Florence thought the red cross could have been made out of something more permanent than tomato ketchup. However, she did think that the white headdress looked very smart, the way it hung down the back to a point.

The pinafore was not so easy. The first of Cicely's efforts completely covered Florence's eyes, although a hole had been made to poke her nose through.

"I can't see where I'm going," she said.

Florence finally agreed that Gloobs could not wear pinafores and settled for an apron as this only covered the lower part of her body and she could see, hear, smell and speak.

Cicely was rather pleased with her efforts until Florence pointed out that the cross was the wrong way and was not supposed to have two noughts either side.

Cicely refused point blank to make another one and Florence had to accept the apron made from an old OXO label.

Florence paraded her uniform all over the tip.

At first, other Gloobs giggled with embarrassment. Young Gloobs marched behind her because they were sure she was advertising some goodies that were being given away.

"FLORENCE GLOOB!" bellowed a voice behind

her and she turned round, "You look ridiculous!" It was her father.

"No I don't!" Florence retorted, "I look like a nurse and that's because I am one."

"What's a nurse?" asked a bystander Gloob as the young Gloobs began to drift away with disappointment.

"I look after the sick," announced Florence with pride.

"That's not very dignified is it!" bellowed Florence's father. (Dignified is another word for posh.) "That's not dignified for a young lady Gloob of your standing."

"I'm standing a lot better than you," Florence retorted as her father fell flat on his face without so much as a warning. Florence ran over to him.

"Father what ever is the matter?"

"Go away I'm sick," he groaned into the mud.

"Why is it three o'clock?" exclaimed Florence, "well now I can nurse you."

"That's the sixth in the last half hour," observed the

bystander Gloob.

"Turn him over and you'll see he's got green spots on his nose," observed another.

"It's the green spotted nose plague," said a third, going cross-eyed trying to look at his own nose before he fell flat on his face.

Quickly Florence organised the bravest Gloobs to become stretcher bearers and collect all the sick Gloobs from all over the tip and bring them to her hospital. There were forty two in all and it was rather cramped but everyone had to admit that Nurse Florence's quick action stopped the spread of the plague.

Her careful nursing, night and day, helped all of the ill Gloobs to recover - including her father.

When they met her in passing, other Gloobs smiled and greeted her with, "Morning Nurse Florence," or "Good afternoon Nurse Florence."

No one ever again dared laugh, not even at the OXO label apron.

2.

How Sherlock Gloob became a Detective.

Ever since they settled on the Tip, Gloobs have been fascinated with the funny things human beings get up to. They have learned a great deal from rubbish discarded (that means thrown away) by humans. How to use money for instance, except that Gloobs do not have any gold so they use coal. To Gloobs it is just as useless.

They have learned to be scientists and invent things and build little factories beneath the tip and make things. Food, for example, became difficult to find on the Tip.

They used to live almost exclusively (that means pretty well 'only') on rhubarb. Well, there was not a lot of rhubarb to be found on the Tip so they organised special 'worker Gloobs' whose job was to leave the tip at night - a terribly adventurous thing to do - and bring food in from a nearby allotment (That's a sort of vegetable garden).

This food, carrots, peas, beans, strawberries, blackberries and, yes, even rhubarb, was processed in the new factories.

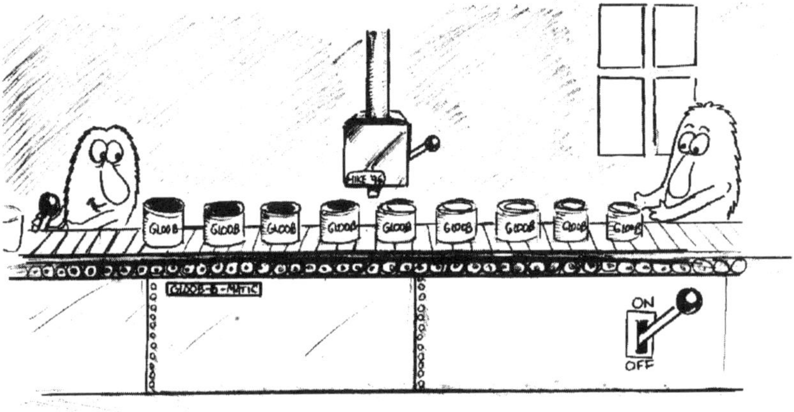

Remember, a garden pea might be small to you but is a meal in itself to a little Gloob. A carrot, well, a carrot is as big as a bus is to you or me. Just think how well we could dine off a bus - if we were given to eating buses!

The factories, which were built underground for the safety of the little Gloob workers, made the fruit and vegetables into all kinds of delightful concoctions which they put into tiny little Gloob tins with tiny little Gloob labels to be sold in the Gloob shops - which were springing up all over the tip. Yet another thing copied from humans.

Of course, Gloobs do not have a clear picture of what human beings look like because they are so big. Gloobs are more interested in what the hairless giants do. (Hairless compared to Gloobs)

Yes, the Community of Gloobs was certainly becoming civilized since they arrived on the Tip - thanks to those very odd creatures called human beings. Odd though they were, it was no where near as odd as the goings on that happened one day on the Tip.

The first to notice it was Sherlock Gloob when he met his best friend Danny Gloob.

Danny had a glazed expression in his eyes and was bouncing about all over the place.

"What's the matter with you?" asked Sherlock Gloob.

Danny was very fond of football. In fact he would play football morning, noon and night - and that is another story.

"I'm a football, I'm a football!" he kept saying.

At first, his friend thought he was being silly and then he saw that he was deadly serious.

"What d'you want to be a football for?" he asked.

"Yes," Danny Gloob answered and bounced away.

"I wonder if his mother knows," muttered Sherlock Gloob.

At exactly that moment, Cynthia Gloob romped across the tip with a large leaf stuck on top of her head.

"Don't tell me," said Sherlock Gloob, "you're a stick of rhubarb."

"Oh how clever of you. Yes I am.! I'm a stick of rhubarb!" she giggled as she romped away , "I'm a stick of rhubarb!"

"Well mind no one bites you!" Sherlock shouted after her. At that point he was knocked off his feet by a rather large Gloob who rolled over him.

"Hey!" he exclaimed, "what do you think you're doing?"

"I'm a big red bus!" cried the Gloob as he rolled on down the Tip.

"Gloobs don't have -" Sherlock Gloob began and then gave up because the 'bus' was out of ear shot, "besides," he muttered to himself, "you happen to be pale green!"

Sherlock Gloob agreed with himself there and then that something was very wrong. Gloobs did not go around thinking they were footballs, sticks of rhubarb or red buses. Not on a normal day they didn't. During the rest of the morning, he met a lamp post that somehow actually lit up, a tin opener trying unsuccessfully to open a can of beans with his teeth and a wheelbarrow being trundled along by a plate of chips. At least the Gloob concerned insisted that he was a plate of chips and he did smell remarkably like it.

Sherlock Gloob was beginning to wonder if he was the only Gloob left on the tip who thought he was a Gloob.

Suddenly, he knew what he had to do. He had to find the answer to the mystery - and that meant, at last, that he could be a detective.

Sherlock Gloob had always wanted to be a detective. That was why he called himself Sherlock. His Parents had called him Charlie but one day, from the gloob library of battered discarded books (that means thrown away) he happened to have read a story entitled 'The Hou—- of the Bask——. Like so many

of the books on the Tip it was incomplete and pages were missing. Charlie, as he was called then, had decided that the story must be entitled 'The House of the Basket' and he had to make up the end for himself. The main thing that came from his reading, however, was the central character who was a clever human being called Sherlock Hol—— . It turned out that he was very good at solving mysteries and catching criminals.

Charlie knew at once that that was what he wanted to do and promptly changed his name to Sherlock.

Immediately, there were two problems. Neither of them any use to Sherlock. The first one was that no one seemed to want a detective because there were no mysteries on the Tip - not that anyone noticed. The second problem was getting use to his new name. Everyone kept calling him either Charlock or Sherlie.

It was not a lot of fun being an out of work detective. Gloobs, on the whole, are very law abiding. They do not go around ignoring sensible rules which are there for the protection and safety of everyone - like many humans do.

He had tried to persuade some of his friends to commit just a little crime so that he could solve it.

"Excuse me," said Harold Gloob, one of Sherlock's close friends, "if I was to commit a crime - which I am not!, how could you solve the mystery if you knew right from the start who did it?"

"I could pretend I didn't know," said Sherlock, "I suppose."

"Why don't you go away and be an actor," said his friend.

So it was that Sherlock was not getting far at being a detective until Danny Gloob came along and insisted that he was a football. Here at last was a mystery of megagloob proportions. Why did Danny Gloob think he was a football? Why did Cynthia Gloob think she was a stick of rhubarb?

When a perfectly normal looking Gloob came up to you and said:

"Hello, I'm a golf club, would you like to play a round of golf with me?" You would think that was a mystery wouldn't you? Well Sherlock was delighted. Now all he had to do was find a partner. Sherlock Hol—- had a doctor for a partner called Doctor What's

On. Sherlock Gloob, therefore, started looking round for some Gloob who did not think that he or she was a screwdriver.

Penelope Gloob was a delightful lemon yellow scatter brain Gloob. She enjoyed life so much that she had no time to remember things. She left things lying around and could not remember where. She got dates mixed up and turned up to friends' birthday parties either three weeks too soon or two weeks too late.

"I say, Penelope old thing," Sherlock greeted her that afternoon. Sherlock thought this was how all detectives talked and he had spent weeks training hard.

Penelope Gloob hit him over the head with her hand bag.

"Old thing yourself!" she shouted back, her feelings hurt.

"What was that for?" asked a shocked Sherlock.

"I'll have you know I'm a lot younger than you!"

"When I said 'Old thing', I didn't mean 'Old thing', I meant 'Old thing'."

She hit him over the head with her hand bag again.

"Stop it!" Sherlock shouted, "I need your help."

"Well stop calling me an old thing then."

"I don't - Oh never mind," said Sherlock as Penelope raised her hand bag once more, "listen Pen old - er - young thing. Don't you think there's something very funny going on, on the Tip?"

"Such as?" asked Penelope Gloob.

"Well, hasn't anyone come up to you lately and told you they were a strawberry mousse?"

"Not lately, no. Caroline Gloob did say she was a clothes line, but I've always thought that's how she wore her clothes."

"Exactly! Self respecting Gloobs do not wear clothes! Unless it's for a special reason. There's a mystery a foot, What's On," said Sherlock, sticking a twisted piece of tubing in his mouth.

"You've got a mysterious foot?" asked Penelope Gloob, "who's What's On and why have you stuck that tube in your mouth?"

"It's not a tube, it's a tobacco pipe. Sherlock Hol—— always smoked a pipe while he was solving a mystery."

"Gloobs do not smoke," said Penelope sternly, "unless their fur catches fire."

"Elementary my dear Penelope," said Sherlock, striking a pose (that means making himself look rather silly). Now we must solve this mystery!"

"I think your the biggest mystery going," said Penelope, about to walk away.

"Wait!" cried Sherlock, "it's my one chance to be a detective!"

Penelope was not impressed and was about to leave him for good when something happened that rather save the day. There was a loud 'ting' behind her which made her jump at least a Gloob and a half high.

She spun round.

"What do you think your doing?!" she shouted at

the little blue Gloob who now stood almost nose to nose with her.

"Ting!" he went into her face, "I'm a triangle!"

"I'll ting your nose if you do that again," Penelope answered him.

"There you are! There you are!" cried Sherlock, "why does everyone think they're not what they really are? It's a mystery, a mystery!"

By this time, the triangle had 'tinged' its way to somewhere else on the tip.

"I'm going to find out what it is," said Sherlock.

"Perhaps they've all had something to drink," Penelope suggested.

"How do we find out?" asked Sherlock.

"You're the detective!" Penelope reminded him.

"Right!" said Sherlock and stuck the pipe in his mouth again.

"I wish you wouldn't do that," said Penelope.

Sherlock ignored her.

"I've got it! We ask as many Gloobs as possible what they had to drink yesterday. Then we come back and study our findings."

It seemed a pretty good idea. So off they went in search of clues.

Sherlock and Penelope had arranged to meet back at Sherlock's little house, a delightful arrangement of chipped flower pots, at tea time.

Sherlock was the first to arrive back at his house with a very miserable look on the end of his nose. This morning, he had been besieged by Gloobs thinking they were all sorts of things, this afternoon, he had not found one.

He sat gloomily staring at his toes. Suddenly, there was a tap at the door. Sherlock opened it and standing there was Penelope Gloob.

"Hello!" she greeted him, "I'm a pound of potatoes!"

"Argh!" exclaimed Sherlock, "not you too!" He

dragged Penelope inside his living room pot while she kept on insisting she was a pound of potatoes.

"Now sit there and be quiet," ordered Sherlock Gloob, pointing to his favourite little armchair. This new problem needed some careful thinking. First of all, Gloobs do not have potatoes by the pound. In fact, one potato is big enough to feed one Gloob for a week. So where had Penelope got the idea of a pound of potatoes?

"Where have you been this afternoon?" asked Sherlock.

"I'm a pound of potatoes," replied Penelope with a satisfied smile on her face.

"Yes, and a very nice pound of potatoes but where have you been this afternoon?!"

For a moment, the glazed look in Penelope's eyes faded and she seemed surprised to find herself in Sherlock's favourite armchair.

"I couldn't find any Gloobs who thought themselves anything but Gloobs," she said.

"Neither could I," Sherlock concurred (that really means 'agreed' in a sort of posh way).

"But then I found out that they all worked in the same food factory inside the Tip. As I was going in, I remember seeing a torn paper bag on the side of which was printed 'A pound of potatoes'. I had been in the factory less than a minute, wondering what the strange smell was, when suddenly, I remember nothing else until now."

"Aha!" exclaimed Sherlock, sticking the pipe in his mouth.

"I wish you wouldn't do that," said Penelope.

"Aha!" exclaimed Sherlock again, ignoring her, "it is elementary my dear What's On."

"I'm not What's On and I'm not sure that I'm your dear either," said Penelope.

"Aha!" exclaimed Sherlock for the third time, "it is clear to me that the answer to the mystery lies in the food factory. I must inform the V.I.G. at once."

The V.I.G., which is short for Very Important

Gloob, is something like the human being's Lord Mayor. He is supposed to organize important occasions and generally sign laws for the health and welfare of the Gloob Community.

The V.I.G. called together all the Boss Gloobs who ran the factories and demanded to know why all Gloobs working for them had suddenly gone funny.

"It's the smell," answered one Boss Gloob.

"Why doesn't it affect you?" asked the V.I.G.

"Because we're the Bosses. We never actually go inside the factories," the V.I.G. was told.

"Then how do you know it is the smell?" the Bosses were asked.

"My Foreman told me," replied one of the Bosses, "just before he decided he was a three wheel bicycle."

"Then the factories must be closed down at once," ordered the V.I.G. and that is exactly what happened.

Within twenty four hours, every Gloob that had been affected had got better.

Professor Offenrite Gloob, the most important scientist on the Tip was called in to find out what the smell was.

"It's Tip gas," he announced.

"What's that?" asked Sherlock Gloob, who was feeling rather proud that his new Detective Agency was becoming quiet famous.

"I don't know," the Professor Gloob replied, "I just made the name up. But it's the cause of all the mystery."

Of course, human beings have know for a long time that Methane gas can collect under Tips. It comes from deep down where the rubbish is rotting. It is highly inflammable (which means it burns very easily) and can kill human beings if they breath a lot of it.

But to little Gloobs it could simply make them think they were something altogether different, like their favourite object - a football or a stick of rhubarb. Sometimes it had been the last thing they had read about before the gas got them, a red bus perhaps or a pound of potatoes.

The factories were rebuilt in gas free areas and everything on the Tip went back to normal.

Sherlock Gloob had a customer for his Detective Agency straight away. Amanda Goob's little son Rupert Gloob had disappeared and was last seen racing across the tip telling everybody he was a jumbo jet - and he had not been anywhere near the Tip gas.

MIKE

3.

The Christmas Story of Albert Gloob.

Albert Gloob had a heart of gold, which means he was very kind and loved doing things for just about everybody. One of the things he loved doing was giving presents to every Gloob that he knew and quite a few that he did not.

Once, he gave a rusty nail as a present. It was his pride and joy. He gave it to little Bollinger Gloob his nephew, for his tenth birthday.

Now, you may think that a rusty nail is not much of a prize possession. However, it happened to be holding up the roof of his house. Five minutes after Albert had left for his nephew's birthday party, his house fell down.

On the occasion of his Aunt Mathilda and Uncle

Bumble Gloob's Silver Wedding, he gave away another of his prize possessions. It was an electroplate on nickel-silver teapot, with a leaky spout. Aunt Mathilda soon found that out, the very first time she used it. The teapot leaked very hot tea all over the large but tender feet of Uncle Bumble.

Then there was the magnificent present of a seagull's egg which he gave to Great Aunt Ermintrude Gloob. He had not meant her to eat it. He thought she would like it as an ornament on her mantelpiece. After all, he had had it on his own mantelpiece for three years.

Great Aunt Ermintrude surprised everyone by being delighted. Then she thought she would enjoy it lightly boiled for her breakfast.

If you have ever tried to eat an egg that was three years old, you will know what Great Aunt Ermintrude Gloob was thinking about her nephew when she cracked open the seagull's egg, (if you have not, then you can only imagine).

It was not surprising, therefore, that very soon, Gloobs began to be very wary of receiving presents from Albert Gloob. (Wary mean suspicious in a careful way). They tended to accept his presents politely and then, after he had left, they buried them on the other side of the tip. If it was a present of food, they fed it to the rats to keep that vermin population down. (Gloobs and rats could not possibly get on - as I will tell you all about one day.)

Albert had no idea, of course, what was happening to his presents. He went on giving them as often as he could.

One day, to his dismay, he discovered that he had no more presents to give. Nor did he have any coal to buy any.

Gloobs had started using coal as money not long after they had arrived on the tip. Back on the rhubarb patch they had not needed money. On the tip, however, they had come in contact with human beings. Money seemed to be very important to humans so Gloobs soon learned what money was used for but not how to make it. Then, Daffy Gloob struck a seam of coal beneath the tip. He was always digging.

The Great Gloob Council thought coal was ideal to use as money. It was too dirty to use as building material and, being dirty, it was only used when absolutely necessary - which was very good for the rate of inflation (I am sure an adult could explain that to you.)

So it was that Albert Gloob found himself without presents to give. What made things worse, Christmas was only a few days away.

Since settling on the tip, Gloobs had learned quickly that humans were strange creatures. It seemed, to them, that only once a year did humans make a real effort to be nice to each other and they called it Christmas. Albert was particularly interested because they gave presents at this time - and, as we know, this was his favourite hobby.

"Oh dear, oh dear, " moaned Albert to himself, "What am I going to do?"

He always gave a Christmas present to Tolly Gloob his best friend whom he had known ever since an awfully long time.

This year, Albert had nothing. Then he had a bright idea. On Christmas Eve, he turned up on Tolly's doorstep as usual. Tolly opened the door.

"Hello," Tolly said, looking all over Albert as if he was glad to see him, but really looking to see what sort of present his friend had brought him this year. Last year it was a broken watch. Albert said it was the best kind because it was never fast or slow.

However, this year, Albert did not seem to be carrying anything.

"Come in," invited Tolly, hoping his voice did not sound too disappointed. After all, even a useless unwanted present was a present.

A whole hour passed of talking about this and thinking about that. Eventually, Tolly could stand it no longer. He decided to give Albert his present. Perhaps it would jog his memory.

"I've got a present for you," said Tolly, springing up from his little armchair. He took a small parcel off the corrugated cardboard sideboard and handed it to his friend.

"I say!" exclaimed Albert, his eyes sparkling with delight, "may I open it?"

"Not until tomorrow morning," Tolly ordered and then sat waiting. A dread began to creep all over Tolly. Here was his friend Albert, the great Present Giver, sitting as if Christmas never existed. What had happened?

Five minutes of complete silence passed. (That is an awfully long time - you try it.)

Suddenly, Albert sat up straight as if he had remembered something.

"Oh yes," he said, "and here's your present."

There was an embarrassing pause.

"Er - where?" asked Tolly.

"Here," said Albert, excitedly, "ME! I'm your Christmas present."

Tolly frowned.

"I beg your pardon?" he asked.

"I'm your Christmas present," Albert repeated.

Tolly could not think of anything to say.

"Don't you think it's a good idea?" asked Albert.

"Well," replied Tolly, "it is rather unusual."

"I think it's a brilliant idea," Albert enthused, "I'm quite valuable really."

"I'm sure you are," observed Tolly, "unique anyway."

"I could do all sorts of things for you round the house. Cleaning, cooking."

"I think I'd rather have a bit of real fresh grown rhubarb," said Tolly, "I mean, I can't very well leave you under the Christmas tree all night, wrapped up in Christmas wrapping paper and unwrap you in the morning, can I?"

Albert thought a moment and then sighed.

"You are right, I suppose," he finally admitted, sadly, "but you see, I haven't got anything else to give."

Tolly then realised that it was a very unselfish thing his best friend had done. He felt guilty about comparing him to a stick of fresh grown rhubarb.

"Look Albert," began Tolly, his nose going bright red - which is the way Gloobs blush, "why do you go around giving presents all the time?"

Albert thought a moment.

"Because it makes me feel all nice inside," he said.

"Well there you are," Tolly pointed out, "it's all very well you feeling nice inside. Your present should make the Gloob you're giving it to feel nice inside as well."

Albert did not quite understand.

"Don't think of yourself when you give a present, think of the Gloob you are giving it to," Tolly explained.

"I never thought of it like that," confessed Albert.

"Well," smiled Tolly, his nose dimming to a rose pink, "you don't have to give me a present this year at all. There's no need."

"There isn't?" Albert blinked.

"No, because in all the ever so long time we've been friends, you've given me the best present ever."

"Really?" Albert exclaimed, his eyes widening. He

began trying to think of all the presents he had given Tolly. Was it the straw hat? The brim had fallen off the first time he wore it. Perhaps it was the half empty fountain pen cartridge? No, on second thoughts, Tolly was not too pleased with that. He had sat on it and dyed his rear fur a bright blue. It took over six months to wash out. Even now he tends never to turn his back on people. Was it the clothes peg he had given him last Christmas? Tolly thought Albert said it was a 'nose' peg and went around for weeks wondering why other Gloobs were looking at him strangely.

"Which present was it I gave you?" asked Albert, finally giving up..

"Why your friendship, you silly Gloob," Tolly explained, "your friendship!"

After that memorable Christmas, Albert always made sure that when he gave a present, it would make the Gloob who received it, feel nice inside.

It was not long before Gloobs on the tip felt honoured to receive a present from Albert Gloob.

4.

The dreadful end of Vanity Gloob.

Vanity and Prudence Gloob had been friends for long before they went to Gloob school together. They were next door neighbours.

Prudence's family lived in the remains of an old wellington boot. Her parents had made it comfortable and tastefully decorated.

Vanity Gloob was brought up next door in a discarded television set that was the envy of that part of the tip. It was palatial (that means like a palace) and extravagant (and that means it cost a lot). Of course, Vanity's parents could afford it because they had a lot of coal in the Gloob Bank. They could also afford to spoil Vanity. What ever she wanted, she had only to ask and she got it.

Prudence, on the other hand, did not want very much. She was happy and knew the difference

between an old wellington that was lovingly cared for and a television set that had umpteen servants to keep out the dirt of the Tip. Prudence was content with just a few things because she had trained herself from being very young never to ask for what she knew her parents could not afford.

So it was that Vanity and Prudence grew up through a strange friendship because they were so completely different.

The older Vanity grew, the sillier she seemed to become and the older Prudence grew, the more serious she became.

She worried about elderly Gloobs whose families had gone away and left them. She organised small groups of young Gloobs to go round doing jobs for them, going errands for them, even providing meals for them in some cases.

Vanity thought only of herself - which is hardly surprising because she spent a great deal of the day sitting looking at herself in a mirror. The car wing-mirror, although cracked, had been installed (that means put in) in Vanity's palace of a house in a place of importance. Vanity made her maid servant clean it every hour on the hour.

Vanity had been given a maid servant for her fourteenth birthday and the poor little Gloob that was unlucky enough to get the job, had a lot to put up with. She would have left months ago but her family needed the coal to pay for important things, like renting the alarm clock case they lived in and, of course, buying food.

The maid's name was Trixie Gloob. She looked forward to the visits of Prudence Gloob because that meant that her mistress Vanity Gloob, would be busy for once, too busy to make her life a misery.

Prudence knew this and tended to make her visits more often than she would have liked.

"That silly Gloob of a maid servant," Vanity would always begin, to impress Prudence, "she can't do anything right."

Vanity was sitting, as usual, at her very fashionable matchbox dressing table.

"I'm sure she does her best, Vanity," said Prudence, trying to defend little Trixie.

"She's hopeless!" exclaimed Vanity Gloob, "I tell her continually to put my brush and comb on the left hand side of my dressing table. See? She can't even do that."

"But it is on the left hand side," said Prudence quietly, knowing full well that Vanity could not tell her left from her right.

"Oh, then it's the other side," Vanity pointed, "I'm always telling her to put it on the other side."

"Why don't you put it on the other side yourself?" Prudence suggested.

"Of course, you would say something like that," snapped Vanity, "I would not expect you to understand my position."

"As far as I can see, it's not a very useful one," observed Prudence Gloob.

"What do you mean?" Vanity demanded.

"Well, you're always sat in front of this mirror. It's a very static sort of position, isn't it," said Prudence.

Vanity Gloob went silent. No one criticised Vanity, not to her face anyway and certainly she did not expect it from her close friend Prudence Gloob.

"I think you had better go," said Vanity Gloob icily to Prudence, "I have a headache coming on."

Prudence knew that that was an absolute lie. However, she did feel sorry for her friend. Prudence had often tried to influence Vanity in the past but had always been unsuccessful. Anyone who is spoilt seldom listens to advice, however good it is.

As Prudence Gloob left the great house, she took Trixie Gloob to one side and made one last effort to get her to leave. No coal in all the Tip was worth putting up with the likes of Vanity Gloob.

It was no use. Trixie shook her head sadly and hurried off as Vanity's shrieking voice echoed through the rooms.

"Trixie! Where are you, you stupid Gloob!? Wait until I get my hands on you!"

Prudence Gloob walked slowly back to her safe, friendly old wellington boot. After that, Prudence never went to visit Vanity Gloob ever again. She felt sorry for poor Trixie Gloob, but, after all, the little Gloob had chosen her own situation and Prudence had greater things to do, like starting a Gloob Cub Pack because she rather fancied the idea of camping.

As for Vanity Gloob, her behaviour became more and more eccentric (and that means really weird). She would stop Gloobs when out shopping and ask them.

"Don't you think I'm beautiful? Have you ever seen anyone as beautiful as me?"

Then she would walk away without hearing the reply - which is just as well because many of them were far from flattering.

Shortly after, she began to change colour, strictly to her own design. Her natural colour was a pale shade of blue but, with the aid of dyes, she developed green stripes, then went purple with yellow spots and every Gloob ran like made because they thought she had caught some dreadful contagious disease.

Finally, came the shoes. Gloobs did not wear shoes. Some wore sensible boots to protect them from the Tip where pieces of broken glass and rusty nails could be quite dangerous.

Vanity had her shoes made specially. The soles were so think they were like stilts. Her shoes were soon to be her undoing. Firstly, they made her stand out above the rest and secondly, she could not run in them at all.

To stand out and not be able to run was fatal when the occasional human being might visit the tip.

One fateful day, as Vanity Gloob was parading herself for all the tip to admire her, a young human girl - who should NOT have been there at all - was picking her way through the rubbish when she gave a delightful cry and bent down to pick up what she thought was a pompom which had been lost or thrown away, a pompom of beautiful orange colour with golden stars in the fur like wool pile.

No one heard Vanity scream for help. In fact, no one ever saw her on the tip again.

It was some months later when news filtered through, said to be from a reliable source. The little human girl had been seen wearing a bobble hat and stitched to it was a gloobish pompom, bright orange with golden stars in the fur-like wool pile.

5.

The cautionary tale of Columbus Gloob

Columbus Gloob could not write, well not very much anyway. He could write his name and that was about it.

He could not read very well either. Little words like 'and' or 'but' were all right, but large words he just did not bother about.

The fault had been when he was very young and preferred sleeping under an empty bean tin, rather than going to school. Even on the few days he did manage to go to school, he always found ways of getting out of having to write - like telling the teacher that a big ant had bitten the index finger of his writing hand and it was all swollen and covered in red and green spots. The teacher was very sympathetic, but if she had told him to wash his hands, the spots would have come off.

Even after he was married, Columbus Gloob managed to keep it a secret from his wife. If ever there was a letter to write, he was somehow extremely busy and his wife had to write it instead.

Not being able to read very well caused worse problems. One day, he got home late from doing nothing in particular on the tip and his wife asked him what he wanted for tea. He said spaghetti on toast, (yet another thing picked up from humans) but as it was her turn to go out on the tip and do nothing in particular, she asked him if he would get it himself, and out she went.

Of course, Columbus could not read the labels on the little Gloob tins, all made at the one and only, brand new Gloob factory under the tip.

His wife was surprised when she returned after a very short turn of doing nothing in particular to find Columbus eating stewed prunes on toast instead. He said he was experimenting with new ideas.

The final disaster came when he told is wife that he was going for a swim in the little pool that the Gloobs used on the far side of the tip.

Half way there, he took what he thought was a short cut (although he had never been that way before). After ten minutes or so he found himself in open country with the tip disappearing behind him.

Surely, he thought, he should be coming to the swimming pool by now? Suddenly, there it was, well not the swimming pool he knew but a much, much bigger pool and not another Gloob in sight. He had it all to himself.

There was a sign there, but he could not read it. So he guessed that it must say, 'SWIMMING POOL, FOR BATHERS ONLY.'

With a happy little cry of delight, Columbus Gloob dived through the air and into the pool.

The shock sent him swimming frantically for the bank on to which he crawled coughing and spluttering.

Now, if you or I had been there, we could have read the sign correctly. It said, 'DANGER. THIS IS A SEWAGE FARM TRESPASSERS WILL BE PROSECUTED.' and if you have ever wondered where those human constructions called 'flush toilets' and drains deposit their contents, that is a sewage farm.

When Columbus returned to the tip, every Gloob within a mile could smell him coming.

After that, no one, except his poor wife, spoke to him.

Finally, Columbus could stand it no longer. He

broke down and confessed to his wife that he could not read properly and that was why he had thought it was a swimming pool.

"Why, you silly old Gloob you," she laughed at him, "why didn't you say so sooner?"

And from that very moment, she began to teach her husband how to write and how to read and he enjoyed every moment of it.

He still had stewed prunes on toast though, because he found that he rather liked that too.

Columbus

6.

The frustrating story of Cornelia Gloob.

Little Cornelia Gloob desperately wanted to run away to join a circus - only Gloobs did not actually have such a thing as a circus.

She had seen a very exciting picture of one. It was a faded poster that had found its way on to the tip. The large glaring letters announced - 'EL VITTORIO'S GIANT CIRCUS' and beneath the letters was a wonderful picture of a man being fired from a cannon.

"Oh I'd love to be fired from a cannon," Cornelia confided to her best friend one day.

"Give you a headache probably," her friend wisely warned her.

"To fly through the air," extolled Cornelia, funny word extol, it means to praise an awful lot, well she was like that.

"Can't think why you want to be fired from a cannon just to fly through the air," said her friend, "every time there's a strong wind Gloobs fly through the air and personally I don't find it much fun because you never know where you are going to land. Besides, being fired from a cannon will probably singe your fur more than like."

"Will you help me to build a cannon and then I can

join a circus."

It took the whole day but eventually, her friend reluctantly agreed to help Cornelia build her cannon.

"What do you build a cannon out of?" asked her friend at the very beginning.

"You have to have a big tube thing that I can fit in."

They searched and found a cardboard tube from the inside of a toilet roll but Cornelia said it was too short.

They found a biro pen without a refill but Cornelia said it was too thin and she did not think she could squeeze one toe into it, let alone her whole self - Cornelia was a rather large Gloob.

They found a piece of rusty exhaust pipe which would have been ideal had it not had a bend in the middle. Cornelia insisted that although many Gloobs thought she already had , she was not ready yet to go round the bend.

Finally they found the ideal piece of tube. It was certainly the right diameter (that means the widest distance across the end of the tube - but then you probably knew that.)

There was, however, one problem. This particular piece of tube had one end buried in the ground and no mount of pulling could get it out.

"How long do you think it is?" asked Cornelia's friend, trying to peer down it only to be met with unfathomable darkness. (I'm not quite sure why we use that word unfathomable like that because sailors measure the ocean in fathoms, like we measure the depth of a hole in metres - but somehow 'unmetrable' doesn't sound right does it? Fathom also means 'to understand', so you work it out.)

"There's another thing," said Cornelia's friend, "what makes you shoot out of the cannon?"

"I'm not sure, but it goes bang I think," replied Cornelia Gloob.

"Do you have to carry your cannon around with you?" asked her friend.

"I suppose so. On the other hand, I could be a

static show." (Static in this case has nothing to do with electricity - it means not moving), "then Gloobs could come and watch me and you could collect the money."

"You mean Gloobs have to pay to watch you pop out of that tube? Do they have to guess where you are going to land?"

"Not really," answered Cornelia Gloob searching amongst some discarded objects not far away. She returned with a toy saucepan which she clamped on the top of her furry round shape.

"Why are you wearing that saucepan?" asked her friend.

"It's not a saucepan any more. It's a crash helmet."

"Oh, so you do intend to crash then?"

"I might," Cornelia replied, "well, now I'm ready."

She began to climb into the tube.

"But we haven't any-" her friend got no further. She was going to say Bang Powder when Cornelia

Gloob disappeared down the tube with a triumphant:

"Wheeeeee!"

It seemed to go on for a very long time, getting fainter and fainter until there was absolute silence.

Cornelia's friend ran over to the tube and shouted down it.

"Hello?!"

There was no answer. I hope at this point you won't mind if I say you should not go near dark holes in the ground, let alone climb into them. You may never ever return.

Cornelia Gloob, however, was very lucky. The little Gloob community had no such thing as an Emergency Rescue Service. Instead, they all gave Cornelia up for good, never expecting to see her again. She did, eventually, turn up three days later on the other side of the tip, hungry, bedraggled (you can imagine what that is like) and in a state of shock

When Cornelia's friend heard of a strange Gloob appearing who's description sounded very familiar, she took the journey to the other side of the tip.

There she found Cornelia, looking much better than she expected.

"Where have you been?" asked her friend.

"In a terrible place!" Cornelia replied, "that tube must be blocked up at once. It goes right down to the heart of the tip. It's dangerous. I thought I would never get out alive!" - and so she went on.

"What about being fired from a cannon?" asked her friend once she got a word in.

"Who ever heard of such a stupid thing!" exclaimed Cornelia Gloob to her friend's great surprise.

Cornelia sat down on the little drum that was firmly wedged between the rusty spokes of an old bicycle wheel. A piece of string hung down from the little drum and did not really look as if it belonged to it.

"Now that reminds me," said Cornelia's friend, seeing the piece of string, "that's just what I need."

She pulled at it but it did not seem to want to

disengage itself from the highly decorated little drum.

Cornelia's friend braced her feet against the wheel rim and gave a huge pull at the string.

Suddenly, there was an enormously loud 'BANG' as the party popper went off and streamers shot high into the air - but highest of all went Cornelia who had been sitting on it all this time. She sailed away above the piles of man-made rubbish eventually to disappear from sight on her second visit to the other side of the tip.

"Oh," commented Cornelia's friend, watching her arch through the sky, "that's how it's done."

7.

The last joke of Hilarious Gloob.

Can you guess how Hilarious Gloob received his name? Hilarious means extremely funny as you may or may not know. Well, the day he was born, his father gave him one look and burst into great peals of laughter. When he had recovered sufficiently, he said:

"That's hilarious!

So the name stuck.

As a baby Gloob, Hilarious did look very funny. Baby Gloobs are usually born covered in soft fur like their parents. Hilarious, however, had no such fur coat. He was almost completely bald all over except for one little tuft on top. So, imagine a ripe plum with eyes, nose, hands and feet and a small cluster of hairs sticking straight up. Visualise, if you can, a punk plum and you have the picture of Hilarious Gloob at birth.

As he grew older, the fur did begin to grow, but in patches. For the first year of his little life, he looked decidedly threadbare and moth eaten. It was not until he had reached his third year that he could claim to have any real fur all over him - and it was green.

Hilarious Gloob was green. Not a quiet, pale, hardly noticeable green that might blend into the back ground, but the loudest, most violent of greens that made the other Gloobs turn their heads away and pretend something had attracted their attention elsewhere.

It was obvious that such treatment would affect Hilarious and it did.

He grew into a notorious practical joker. We all know that some practical jokes are harmless fun - such as putting a black plastic beetle in someone's First Course of garlic mushrooms at dinner when they are not looking. Practical jokes, however, have a danger of growing into monstrous and harmful things.

When Hilarious first began his habit of practical joking, he was at Gloob school. The jokes were fairly ordinary, like putting a whoopee cushion on the teacher's chair. Then the jokes began to develop.

One day, he found a small piece of cotton wool which had blown on to the tip. He cleaned it up, fluffed it into a ball. He searched about the tip for bits to represent eyes, nose and feet and then introduced it to his friend as Esmeralda Gloob, a little girl Gloob from the other side of the tip.

His friend, Jeremy Gloob, who was a little short sighted, fell in love with the ball of cotton wool, thinking that it was a shy young thing who did not like talking very much.

There followed three hours of a one-sided conversation by Jeremy. He declared his undying love to the ball of cotton wool while Hilarious Gloob and a small band of like-minded Gloobs watched in secret, hardly able to suppress their laughter.

When a slight puff of wind blew Esmeralda's nose off, Jeremy was horrified. When her left eye popped out and rolled away, he began to be very suspicious. He looked very closely at Esmeralda and realised that she was not what she seemed. At that point, the hidden group of his 'school mates' rolled out of their hiding place unable to contain their laughter any longer.

Jeremy never spoke to Hilarious ever again for making him such a public fool and, unfortunately, Hilarious could not have cared less.

As he grew older, his practical joking began to take on an unpleasant turn - as practical joking often does. He found great but twisted pleasure from knocking on the doors of Gloob's houses and then running a short distance to hide and watch the angry and frustrated Gloobs come to their doors to find no-one there.

What he chose not to see was the fear he caused to many of the elderly Gloobs whose door he thundered on late at night. Nor did he worry himself about the elderly Gloobs who struggled to the door in great pain - because elderly Gloobs can suffer from arthritis too - only to find that their tearful efforts to answer the door were fruitless because there was no visitor on their little doorsteps.

Finally, however, Hilarious Gloob made a big mistake. He was very fond of pulling chairs away from behind unsuspecting Gloobs who, immediately upon trying to sit down on the absent chair, would end up on the floor. Gloobs are round and fluffy and therefore do not suffer injuries like human beings. Human beings have been known to damage their spines and be paralysed for life because another human being pulled a chair away from behind them, just as they were sitting down. I hope that you do not do that trick. It is very, very dangerous.

On the day he made his big mistake, Hilarious Gloob planned to pull the chair away from behind a very, very important Gloob who was giving a speech at a very important meeting.

Hilarious Gloob's mistake, however, was telling his only remaining friend what he planned to do.

So it was that on that fatal day, just as the Very Important Gloob was ending his speech, Hilarious Gloob pretending he was part of the Very Important Gloob's bodyguard, pulled the chair away from behind him.

The Very Important Gloob sat down and found himself falling backwards. Hilarious Gloob howled with laughter from the place where he had run to hide. One or two Gloobs in the audience giggled too, but some realised that something terrible had gone wrong.

The Very Important Gloob began to roll uncontrollably down the slope behind the platform from which he had made his speech.

He continued to roll and the giggling in the audience stopped. Even Hilarious Gloob's laughter died away as he watched the Very Important Gloob continue to roll down the slope and finally fall into the swift flowing stream at the bottom. The black unwholesome water flowed round the edge of the tip and away into country that Gloobs never dared enter.

A terrible silence fell upon the assembled Gloobs until a group of brave would be little heroes jumped up and ran down the slope. They searched the banks of the swift flowing stream and returned later to say that no trace of the Very Important Gloob could be found. But Hilarious Gloob was found, cowering in his hiding place.

He was dragged forth and duly arrested. His trial was short and snappy. He was accused of willfully playing a practical joke on the person of the Very Important Gloob, which had resulted in the disappearance and undoubted end of the said Very Important Gloob.

"I didn't, I didn't," wailed Hilarious Gloob, "it wasn't me! It wasn't me!"

But the prosecution brought out their prize witness, the one and only friend he had. His so called friend told the Court everything that Hilarious Gloob had told him - confidentially.

"It's a lie!" cried Hilarious Gloob.

"Silence!" shouted the Gloob Judge.

“I saw him do it,” called out a member of the jury.

“Do you think you should be on the jury?” demanded the lawyer Gloob for the defense.

“It doesn’t matter,” the Gloob Judge retorted, “he’s obviously guilty.”

“Oh,” said the lawyer Gloob for the defense and sat down.

“It only leaves me to pass judgement,” said the Gloob Judge, “I pronounce that you be found guilty as charged and shall be locked away for the rest of your life in - THE OXO TIN!”

Hilarious Gloob fainted. Such a harsh sentence was too much to bare.

The Oxo Tin was a source of abject terror (and that’s pretty awful terror) to all Gloobs. Gloob mothers frightened their Gloob children with it if they were naughty.

“If you don’t behave yourself you’ll end up in the Oxo Tin!”

And so, the unconscious Hilarious Gloob was dragged away.

He finally regained consciousness, held between a couple of burly Gloobs standing before the very dreadful shape of the Oxo Tin. It towered above him, rusting and waiting, airless and dark.

The two burly Gloobs remained standing, silently. At last, Hilarious Gloob could stand it no longer.

"What are we waiting for?" he demanded, "why don't you lock me away then?!"

"We're waiting for the gaoler," replied one of the guards.

Five more minutes of waiting past and then, to Hilarious Gloob's surprise, the guards released him and, with a steady march about, they disappeared into the rising mist that so often clung to the tip.

Hilarious Gloob was alone. He shivered and tried to make himself into as small a ball as possible for comfort and warmth.

Why had they deserted him? Where was the gaoler?

As these thoughts were going through his mind and also, it must be confessed, the idea of escape, Hilarious saw the shape of a Gloob coming slowly towards him through the mist. There was something a little frightening about the shape. It glowed.

Hilarious Gloob began to tremble. Even more violently as the shape came closer and he recognised the features of the Very Important Gloob.

But what terrible features. They were covered in green slime and the dark eyes were clearly the awful eyes of a ghost.

Hilarious Gloob screamed and fell forward on his face.

"I didn't mean to do it," he blubbered, "I did not mean to do it."

The dreadful spectre opened the specially secured door cut into the side of the Oxo Tin and beckoned him towards the dark entrance of doom.

Hilarious Gloob was crying hysterically and screaming that he would never ever play a practical joke again.

The frightening vision of the Very Important Gloob waited silently and then began to giggle. His giggles were added to by further giggles from behind the Oxo Tin.

Suddenly, Gloobs began appearing from all directions. Everyone was laughing. They were all laughing at Hilarious Gloob. At the front of them all, holding their furry sides, stood the Gloob Judge and members of the jury, plus everyone who had ever had a practical joke played on them by Hilarious Gloob. Stepping out of the crowd came his one and only friend. It was he who had decided, as soon as he knew of Hilarious Gloob's plan, that Hilarious needed teaching a lesson.

His one and only friend had told the Very Important Gloob what Hilarious intended to do and the Very Important Gloob told his friend the Gloob Judge. Between them, they set up the whole thing. The Very Important Gloob pretended to fall backwards into the stream and drown, although he was a very good swimmer and climbed out further down the bank to turn up later made up as a very convincing ghost. Now that it was all over, he was busy cleaning himself up.

Hilarious Gloob's one and only friend went over to the distressed heap and lifted him gently to his feet. Hilarious looked with bewilderment into the smiling faces of the Gloobs around him.

"Now, Hilarious," said his one and only friend, "now you know what it is like to be on the receiving end of a nasty practical joke. And we hope you never play one on any Gloob - friend or otherwise - ever again."

And do you know, he never did - or at least I never heard that he did.

8.

The tale of the first and last Pirate.

You would not think that Gloobs could be pirates, would you. Not real live, throat-cutting, blood-thirsty pirates. Gloobs are normally so well rounded, so to speak, and besides, there are no seas or oceans on the tip.

However, that did not seem to matter to little Jeremy Gloob. He had read at least six pages of a very battered book entitled 'Treasure Island'. Six pages does not sound a lot but it was enough to make Jeremy want to be a pirate.

"Hello Jeremy," greeted his best friend Amanda Gloob.

"I'm not Jeremy," he told her.

"Well you used to be."

"I'm Black Jake the Pirate."

"You're not black, you're lemon yellow," Amanda retorted, wondering what on earth had got into her friend, "is that why you're dressed funny? And what's a pirate anyway?"

Three days it had taken him to find the right things to make him look like a pirate. A black leather belt, a home-made wooden sword, little wellingtons (which meant stretching his almost non-existent legs), a patch for his left eye - only he could not see very well with it covering his eye so he wore it above it. Finally, everything was topped with a resplendent bicorn hat with a skull and crossbones on it.

Jeremy's eyes glazed over.

"A pirate sails the Seven Seas."

"Well that puts the lid on it for a start," muttered Amanda, "hang on though."

She left Jeremy for only a minute or two as the glaze faded from his eyes. She returned rolling a white plastic tub with a red screw top lid.

"There," she said, as she up ended it in front of him "though why you want to sail round that I can't imagine."

"What's that?" asked Jeremy.

Amanda read the label.

"Seven Seas Cod Liver Oil Capsules."

"I don't think a pirate sails round a tub of cod liver oil capsules!" snapped Jeremy, "I need a boat so's you can walk the plank."

"I don't think I like the sound of that," said Amanda, "well if you need a boat, you'll have to go down to the brook."

The brook was a dirty, muddy mess that flowed round the base of the tip from a direction that no one knew, to a direction that no one wanted to know.

It was quite deep and quite wide where it touched

the tip.

"Right!" shouted Black Jake, the would-be pirate, "then let's go me hearties."

"Your what ?" asked Amanda, following him with a sigh of frustration.

Black Jake stopped at the edge of the murky, evil smelling brook.

"Wonderful!" he exclaimed and Amanda gave him an odd look, "all we need now is a boat."

"WE? I don't want to be a pirate!" Amanda told him firmly.

"I can't be a pirate on my own," Black Jake pointed out, "I need someone to walk the plank."

"What is this 'walk the plank'?" asked Amanda.

"You'll see," said Black Jake, "help me find a boat."

"What about that over there?"

Amanda Gloob pointed to a stout looking shoe box.

"Great! But it's a bit big."

"That?" She pointed to the discarded inside of an empty matchbox.

"Too small," decided Black Jake, "but that will do nicely." He pointed to the bottom half of an old tobacco tin that had become separated from its lid.

"It's made of tin," said Amanda, "it will sink."

"I bet it won't," announced Black Jake the Pirate Gloob, "help me get it into the water."

Sceptically, (that means she did not believe it would float), Amanda helped the would-be pirate drag the tobacco tin down to the brook's edge.

"Now we need a piece of string to tie to it so that it doesn't float away," said Black Jake.

"Or drag it back up off the bottom," mumbled Amanda.

Once the string was tied to it, the 'boat' had to be pushed off the bank and into the water. It was not easy for two little Gloobs but finally, with the tiniest of splashes, they did it.

Black Jake the Pirate had proved himself very wise because the current did catch the tin, which did float and would have sailed away had he not tied it up to a useful root sticking out of the bank.

"Now," said Black Jake, "we need a sail."

"What is that?"

"When the wind blows, it makes the boat go where you want it to."

"You hope," murmured Amanda

Black Jake the Pirate was not going to argue. He searched until he found a piece of wood that would make a very good mast. Amanda was ordered at the same time, to find a piece of material to make a sail. She had found eight pieces before Jeremy Gloob was satisfied and on the remnant of stiff cotton handkerchief, he drew a skull and crossbones like he had seen in the book and, earlier, had drawn on his hat. Only this time he painted the design with thick oozy black mud from the brook.

Fixing the mast into the 'boat' really was a problem.

By this time, the word had spread that something interesting was going on down by the brook and a little group of Gloobs had assembled to watch.

"Why d'you think he's dressed like that?" asked one onlooker.

"Search me. Is he one of us?"

"He looks like a Gloob. I think he used to be Jeremy."

"What's he doing?"

"Sitting in a tin."

"Sorry I asked."

"He says he's making a boat. He's got to fix that stick, with the bit of cloth on, so that it stays upright."

"What ever for?"

No one was quite sure.

"Bang a hole in the tin," some Gloob shouted, "and push it through."

"The water would come through as well wouldn't

it?!" the pirate snapped back, rather annoyed that his idea had become something of a side show.

"Here!" shouted another, "try this!"

The Gloob that had shouted was rolling an object down the bank towards the boat. His antics (that means the way he was behaving) were very odd. He seemed to be treating the object with great respect and then, every so often, he would stop and lick his fingers. When he got it to the water's edge, he shouted a warning.

"Don't get it on your fur, you'll never get it off!"

"What is it?"

"I don't know, but it tastes quite nice."

Very carefully, the piece of sticky toffee was got into the boat and did a wonderful job of fixing the mast into the bottom of the tobacco tin.

"NOW!" exclaimed Black Jake gleefully, "all we need now is a plank."

"Will this do?" asked Amanda. She had found a

lollipop stick earlier and just knew it would come in for something.

"The very thing!" exclaimed Black Jake the Gloob Pirate, "all he have to do is fix it so that it sticks out over the side of the boat."

"Over the water?"

"Yes."

"What ever for?"

"You'll see," said Black Jake.

The lollipop stick was firmly tied across the tin with one end, as Black Jake insisted, sticking out over the edge.

"It makes a very nice seat," announced Amanda, sitting on it and bouncing up and down.

"You're not supposed to sit on it," said Black Jake, "you're supposed to walk on it."

"Where to?" asked Amanda.

"Just stand on it," Black Jake instructed.

To humour him, because after all he was her friend, she did as she was told.

"Now what?" she inquired.

"Aha me hearties!" Black Jake cried at the top of his voice.

"I beg your pardon?" Amanda asked politely.

"That's how pirates speak," said Black Jake.

"How odd," Amanda commented.

"Shiver me timbers ye lily livered varmint!"

"Is that more pirate talk?"

"Yes," said Black Jake, "now please don't interrupt any more!"

Jeremy Gloob drew out his sword.

"Now WALK!" he demanded, putting on the worse scowl he could think of.

"WALK WHERE?!" Amanda asked, getting quite cross with Jeremy's strange behaviour, "and why are you pulling your face like that?"

The gentle Jeremy she knew had changed character completely and now she was beginning to feel very uncertain of her situation.

Black Jake drew out his sword and stabbed it at Amanda. She gave a little squeak and stepped back along the plank.

“Aha!” shouted Black Jake and stabbed at her again.

“Jeremy Gloob! What are you- ooh!” and Amanda Gloob stepped backwards off the end of the plank.

SPLOSH! She landed in the gruesome brook and was immediately swept away.

Luckily, however, Amanda was an excellent swimmer and was able to scramble ashore.

Black Jake was giving his worse scowl ever at the surrounding crowd of onlookers.

“Who’s next?” he shouted, lifting his sword above his head. Within the split fraction of a second, he was alone except for a soggy and furious Amanda who was bearing down on him.

"What do you think you are playing at, Jeremy Gloob?" she demanded.

"I'm not playing at anything," Black Jake retorted, the scowl having become permanent.

"Well you can 'not play at anything' on your own then!" Amanda announced very firmly and, turning her back on her one time friend, she marched away out of sight over a rise of ground.

A final big sneeze followed her departure and he really was alone.

"I don't care!" shouted Black Jake, waving his sword above his head, "pirates don't need friends!"

Black Jake the Pirate, who once upon a time used to be the lovable Jeremy Gloob, sat in his boat and planned his next move.

He did not think he could go as far as really using his sword to hurt anyone, but he had to be a real pirate or not at all.

According to the tatty six pages of Treasure Island which he had read, pirates got their treasure from robbing other ships on the high seas - well it would have to be the murky brook. Now that might present a problem, he thought.

Suddenly, his eyes lit up. The Ferry!

Shortly after the Gloob Community had settled on the tip, they had learned some of the ways of human beings. One of them was the use of money, except that they decided to use tiny lumps of coal. Coal, they discovered was useless and therefore must be valuable. But it was also messy and so a Bank was opened that took the coal in and issued Gloob printed money instead.

The safety of the Bank was very important, so its owners found the best suitable object in which to set it up. It was an old gas fire. It had lots of hidden cavities where the tiny bags of coal could be stored securely.

The gas fire, unfortunately, was on the wrong side of the murky brook and so a ferry boat had to be built to carry Gloobs and their 'money' across it.

"That's it," said Black Jake, his eyes shining, "stop

the ferry and threaten them with walking the plank if they didn't hand over their money."

It seemed so simple. The ferry was further down the brook, round the bend where the water was equally deep and equally wide.

Black Jake the Pirate set sail in eager anticipation (don't those two words sound nice, but behind them lay a sinister purpose).

As he rounded the bend in the brook, the little raft like ferry was already half way across the dark water, the Ferrygloob paddling hard to keep them on a straight course against the current.

There were three Gloobs on the ferry going to the Bank, clutching their little bags of coal.

"HOVE TO, YE VARMINTS!" shouted a voice, "AND PREPARE TO HAND OVER YOUR TREASURE!"

The little Ferrygloob nearly fell off the ferry when he saw the tobacco tin bearing down upon them. There was a little bump and Black Jake drew out his sword.

"You hand your treasure over, or you walk the plank!" snarled Black Jake.

Every Gloob on the tip had heard about poor Amanda Gloob's terrible experience of 'walking the plank' and so they handed over their little bags of coal without further protest.

Black Jake let the ferry sail on and he paddled his tobacco tin back up stream to his own anchorage, where he tied up his boat.

He took out the three little bags of coal and like a true pirate, he buried them, deciding to draw a map later.

"Well that was easy," he said to himself, "I'll have a nap and try again."

And he did try again. When he woke up, he set sail.

To his surprise, the ferry raft was full to almost sinking with Gloobs. They must not have heard about the dreaded Black Jake, pirate of the murky brook.

Once again he threatened them with walking the plank and gleefully took the little bags off them. They felt heavier than usual which made Black Jake grin even wider at the thought of all that coal. He was about to sail back to his hiding place when he saw that the ferry had quickly returned to the side of the brook and another load of Gloobs were getting on, each one of them carrying a large bag full of coal.

Although his boat was already low in the water, he could not let such treasure get away. He waited as the ferry was paddled towards him.

This did seem very easy.

"Hand over your-" he began and before he could finish, all the Gloobs on the ferry had queued up to give him their little bags.

Well, he thought, his reputation must really have got around. He was a real pirate now. As they handed him their treasure, he heaved them behind him into his tin boat. The last bag to be given him seemed the heaviest of the lot,

So much treasure! So much -!

Suddenly, Black Jake felt his feet go cold. He looked down and saw why. Dirty brook water was filling the bottom of his boat. The bags of treasure had been so heavy that the tobacco tin had sunk lower and lower until the brook began to lap over the sides. As more water poured into the boat, it began to sink and with it, Black Jake and all his treasure.

He floundered in the current, but he was a fairly strong swimmer and dived beneath the murky, muddy water to find his treasure.

He surfaced, gasping for breath, dragging one bag after another until he was too tired to look for any more.

Shivering, his fur soaked through and clinging to him, he climbed up the bank of the brook for the last time and collapsed but not before he had shouted:

"You're not getting your treasure back!"

The Gloobs that he had robbed had strange amused looks on their faces.

"We don't want it, thanks," said one.

Black Jake the Pirate frowned and sat up. He picked up one of the bags and struggled with the string round the neck. As the knot gave way, the contents emptied all over the floor at his feet. He stared in disbelief. Instead of treasure, he saw big rocks and stones. That was why the bags had been heavier than usual.

"You didn't think we'd really let you get away with it," said another Gloob.

"When we knew what you were up to, we decided to

fill our bags with rocks," said a third.

"And let you rob as many as your greedy eyes felt like," said a fourth.

"And that sank your boat and serves you right for thinking up such a silly idea," said a fifth.

Black Jake the Pirate had not quite given up. There was the real treasure he had buried.

He smiled to himself, but the smile soon faded when he saw Amanda Gloob join the circle around him. In her hands were the three bags he thought were in a secret and safe location.

"We also followed you and saw where you buried these," said Amanda, giving them back to the Gloobs they belonged to.

Black Jake looked a sad mess. He had lost his hat and his sword. His little boat was at the bottom of the brook.

Amanda went up to him and took hold of his hand.

"Now," she said, "just who are you? Black Jake the

Pirate or Jeremy Gloob?"

He looked down at himself and then at Amanda. A big grin spread across his face.

"Jeremy Gloob," he said. And that is who he was ever after.

9.

The Theatrical Tale of Tilly Gloob.

"Hi am goin' on the stage!" announced Tilly Gloob one day to her best friend Dorathea Gloob.

"What stage?" asked her friend who was picking bits of grit out of her fur. It had been a particularly windy day and that meant grit.

"The stage."

"Have we got one?" asked her friend.

Tilly thought a moment.

"It's in a theatre."

"Have we got one of those?" asked Dorathea Gloob.

"I'll find one," Tilly Gloob announced firmly and she marched off in search of one.

"Don't think she knows what a theatre looks like," said Dorathea Gloob, far more interested in the grit in her fur.

She was right. Tilly had no idea what the outside of a theatre looked like. She had collected lots of scraps of posters and drawings and even bits of writing about the inside of a theatre but not the outside. She had never heard of a Gloob theatre anywhere on the Tip.

"That must be because it looks like an ordinary Gloob house," she said to herself.

Of course, there is no such thing as an ordinary Gloob house. They come in all shapes and sizes from sauce bottles to old fridges, cast off ladies handbags to gutted T.V. sets.

She chose a rusting alarm clock case for her first call. She knocked politely.

A small grubby looking Gloob peered out from the back.

"Wotcher want?" he asked her, his large eyes narrowing suspiciously.

"Is this a theatre?" asked Tilly Gloob.

"Only when dad gets home," replied the little grubby Gloob and he disappeared.

"What kind of answer's that?" asked Tilly, then she found out.

"Aha!" exclaimed a very dramatic voice behind her, "what is this I see before me. A damsel in distress?"

"Eh?" Tilly retorted, turning round in surprise. She always thought a damsel was a sort of plum.

"A dream that trips the weary Tip in search of a long lost mother. Ah, I see it all in three Acts and a curtain call."

Tilly found herself facing a large blue tinted Gloob wearing a vast floppy hat with an enormous brim. From under the hat, at the back, a long piece of black silk with red lining flowed down to the ground. It was the nearest thing a Gloob could get to a cloak because as we all know, Gloobs are not built like humans and do not have shoulders.

Tilly pointed at the rusty clock case.

"Is this a theatre?" she asked.

"Dear me no," replied the blue tinted Gloob dramatically, "that is the residence of me and my family. (He meant that was where he lived.)

"Where's the theatre then?" inquired Tilly.

"Theatre? What would you want with the theatre?" He pronounced it The-a-tor and made his cloak swirl in a very authoritarian manner (That means bossy.)

"I'm going on the stage to be an actress," Tilly Gloob informed him, "Two beans or not two beans that is the question," She quoted her favourite line from a famous human play that she had discovered in the newly set up Gloob library of tattered and slug-eaten books, posters and pamphlets carefully collected from various parts of the Tip.

"Are you any good?" asked the blue tinted Gloob.

"I don't know. I've never been on the stage before. Once more put on your breeches dear friends, once more, and cover the holes up with that stale bread! Where is the theatre then?" Tilly waved her arms about because that is what she thought actors should do when they acted. "Alas poor Horlicks, he's down a well."

"I suppose I could try you out," said the blue tinted Gloob, dodging a fairly vicious swipe by Tilly Gloob who was really getting into the part, "come along to the theatre this afternoon for an audition." (That is when you show the person in charge what you can do and that person tells you if what you can do is any good) "Just ask for Sir Garrick O'Gloob Gloob."

Certain Gloobs who thought themselves important had started using human titles like 'Lord' and 'Sir'. Great actors, they thought, were all called 'Sir' - just like teachers, although they did not really know why.

"But where is the theatre?!" yelled Tilly at Sir Garrick O'Gloob Gloob as if he was hard of hearing and not all there.

"Everybody knows where the the-a-tor is," announced Sir Garrick and he disappeared with a swirl of his cloak into his residence.

"I DON'T!" shouted Tilly after him but it was too late. She half thought of knocking on his door but decided against it. Instead, she stormed away angrily to find someone who would be more helpful.

The first Gloob she met was not at all helpful.

"Theatre? Oh yes, that's where they put you on a table like the main course at a restaurant and carve things off you- or set your nose if you happen to break it." He meant the Operating Theatre in the Gloob Memorial Hospital of course. "Have you broken your nose then?"

"No I haven't" retorted Tilly, wondering what on earth the silly Gloob was talking about.

"It's always looked like that then has it?"

Tilly Gloob stormed away again. She was very good at storming away. This time she was muttering dark words under her breath. If you are not sure what dark words are, then perhaps I ought not to explain except that they contain expressions like 'idiot', 'arm pot' 'dosey nut' and other things.

The next Gloob Tilly met looked more promising. Remember, I only said looked.

"Let me see now," said the rather faded lady Gloob who wore a large paper hat with dead flowers on it (They looked remarkably as if they had once been dandelions) "Oh yes, I remember going there to see a play called 'Ten Gloobs in a tin box.'"

Tilly brightened up. If this Gloob had been to see a play at the theatre, then she must know its whereabouts.

"So you know where it is then?"

"The tin box?"

"The theatre," said Tilly, feeling her temperature rising.

"Didn't think much of the play," commented the Gloob in the hat.

"Were the actors that bad?"

"Don't know. Never saw any. They were inside the tin box all the time."

"But where is the theatre?" shouted Tilly whose nose began to glow.

"I haven't the faintest idea, dear," said the paper hatted Gloob, "I'm useless at directions. In fact, I've spent all morning trying to find out where I live!"

Tilly - yes, Tilly stormed away.

Finally, it was not the asking for directions that found her the theatre, it was one of her 'storming aways'. The last one in fact.

She stormed away after being told she ought to know better than to go on to the stage. It was not the sort of thing young lady Gloobs did. Tilly had stormed away from the silly Gloob that had said it and found herself outside a large upside down wooden crate stamped with the curious words 'BEST BANANAS', only written upside down of course. Tied to one corner was a piece of cardboard which announced THE GLOOB HIPPODROME, when it stopped flapping. (The cardboard, not the Hippodrome.)

Tilly found the Stage Door and went in.

"Yes?" asked an officious voice before she had taken many steps. Just inside the Stage Door was a very elderly looking Gloob wearing a much worn peak cap on which was the motto 'Stage Door Keeper'.

"I've come for an audition," Tilly announced.

"Who says?" asked the Stage Door Keeper Gloob.

"I do," Tilly retorted. (That means answered back rather sharply.)

"What are you auditioning for?" asked the Stage Door Keeper.

"Because I want to," Tilly snapped back beginning

to get a little impatient.

"No, I mean what part are you auditioning for?" asked the Stage Door Keeper as if Tilly was rather lacking in the brains section.

"I don't know because Sir Garrick O'Gloob Gloob didn't say."

"Oh him," sniffed the Stage Door Keeper Gloob, "go on through there."

Tilly Gloob entered the fantasy world of the theatre. Curious pieces of scenery hung around her. Costumes littered the floor in a very untidy way.

There was no lighting like human theatres because Gloobs had not yet discovered the use of electricity and gas or naked candles were unthinkable in such a confined space as a wooden box where everything was very burnable - and that included the fur of little Gloobs! So all performances were done during the afternoon hours of daylight. In the Summer, an additional performance was given in the evening. Daylight was collected from the wide gaps between the planks of the crate walls and reflected by discreet little mirrors on to the stage (which means that the mirrors could not be seen by the audience.)

The roof was solid so that if it rained, it did not soak the audience. However, it did tend to make a terrible noise and drown the actors - in another sense.

Tilly stood quietly in the wings of the Gloob Hippodrome listening and watching the performance on stage.

Sir Garrick O'Gloob Gloob was being very

theatrical. As you know, Gloobs cannot stride about because they have very short legs so they tend to shuffle or hop instead. Sir Garrick O'Gloob Gloob hopped with tremendous dignity from one point on the stage to another. He delivered his lines in a great voice.

"Say not that you are" - hop - "but will be soon" - hop - "should you find it as it is!" - hop.

Tilly could not make head nor tail of what the great Actor was saying. She was sure that a lot of the audience did not either because a good half of them were asleep.

"When it is," hop "or shall be," hop - went on Sir Garrick O'Gloob Gloob.

At that precise moment, it happened.

For realism on stage, the scenery designer had placed a single stub of a candle lit to represent the sacrificial flame of something or other. He had sworn to everyone that it was quite safe. However, the piece of paper scenery closest to it had begun to smoulder and suddenly burst into flames making Sir Garrick O'Gloob Gloob hop much higher than he had ever done in his life before.

Those who were awake in the audience thought that the play was getting somewhere at last and began to applaud the special effects.

Slowly, they realised that the theatre was now pretty thoroughly on fire and made panic dashes for the emergency exits. Those on and nearest the stage were the first out, including Tilly.

The newly formed Gloob Fire Brigade was called. They had not been in existence very long and this was their first major fire. They had not got as far as having a fire engine yet. It was being built. Neither did they have hose pipes because they were not sure what to make them out of. They did have little buckets. They set up a chain of helpers that stretched from the dark water stream, at the foot of the Tip, to the now cheerfully burning theatre.

I know that you are clever enough to realise that it took a long, long time for the tiny amounts of water to reach the conflagration because most of it got spilt on the way. (Now there's a magnificent word. Conflagration. It means a great burning.)

Soon there was nothing left of the Gloob Hippodrome but a black charred heap, so everyone went home and the Fire Brigade returned to its Headquarters satisfied with an afternoon's work and ever more determined to find a way to make hose pipes.

Just before Tilly was about to leave the scene of all the excitement, a very bedraggled Sir Garrick O'Gloob Gloob stopped her. (Do you really need bedraggled explained or can you use your imagination?)

"Ah the dear little Gloob who wants to be an actor, to tread the magic stage of make believe."

He looked rather watery eyed at the smouldering mound.

"Fear not!" he exclaimed, "we shall see a new theatre rise from the ashes and you shall have your audition."

"Well thank you very much," said Tilly very politely, "it doesn't actually matter any more. You see, I've changed my mind. I don't want to be an actor any more. I want to be a Fireman, it's far more dramatic!" - and she trotted off to find the Fire Station.